# Stallion Or Stud?

Copyright © 2005 Bishop Marshal L. Thomas
All rights reserved.
ISBN: 1-4196-0743-X

To order additional copies, please contact us.
BookSurge, LLC
www.booksurge.com
1-866-308-6235
orders@booksurge.com

BISHOP MARSHAL L. THOMAS

# STALLION OR STUD?

## THE CONCEPT

2005

# Stallion Or Stud?

# CONTENTS

| | |
|---|---|
| Dedication | ix |
| Introduction | xiii |
| **Chapter 1** Freedom from Conformity | 1 |
| **Chapter 2** Nature of the Species | 5 |
| **Chapter 3** The Stud | |
| Role, Characteristics and Traits | 9 |
| **Chapter 4** The Stallion | |
| Role, Characteristics and Traits | 15 |
| **Chapter 5** Doomed to Stud or | |
| Or Destined to be a Stallion | 19 |
| **Chapter 6** Leaving a Legacy | 27 |
| **Chapter 7** Men, What can we do? | 33 |

*I Dedicate This Book To My Loving Wife, Patricia A. Thomas Who Has Been Very Patient And Supportive Of My Work. As God Has Unfolded This Particular Book Through Me To Share With The World, Her Support Has Been Invaluable. To My Daughter, Marsha D. Thomas Turnes And To My Grandchildren, Kayla D. Thomas, Joseph K. Turnes Jr., And James Marshal Turnes Whose Presence Has Contributed To My Desire To Spread The Message Of This Book.*

*To My Mother, Mary C. Thomas Who Has Always Been Happy For The Achievements Of Her Children; Thank You Mother For Your Strength And Courage. To My Baby Brother, Minister Samuel C. Thomas Thank You For Your Support And Constant Encouragement To This Project. To All Of My God Children For Always Believing In Me. A Special Dedication Is Sent To My Aunt Marva Fears For Keeping Me Positive When It Seemed That Everyone Was Against Me. To My Secretary And Reader, Ms. Sharon D. Mcginnis For Assisting Me In The Composition Of This Book. Thank You For Your Hard*

*Work And The Time You Committed To This Project. Also, To Ms. Africa Olitta, Thank You For Also Helping Me With The Composition Of This Book. To James And Jackie Hale For The Information You Shared With Me. To My Long Time Friend, Bishop Noel Jones For Your Prolific And Inspiring Words Of Knowledge Along With My Spiritual Brothers, Dr. Wallace Williams And Daryl Coley, Overseer Joshua Paul Logan. To my God Father, Rev. E. J. Brown. Thank You For Being There For Me*

*In Loving Memory*
*I Also Wish To Dedicate This Project In Loving Memory Of My Deceased Family. My Father, Bishop Sherman (Hammer) Thomas, Who Preached And Taught The Words Of Righteousness And Honesty To Me Through The Word Of God. And To My Grandmother, Everlina Montgomery, Who Raised Me And Encouraged Me To Continue My Education. Her Memories Are So Precious In My Heart! My Grandfather And Grandmother Bishop Perry And Mother Rosetta Thomas, Both Left A Legacy That Will Never Be Forgotten. My Mother-in-law Mother Evelyn (Fat Momma) Byers, The Greatest Mother-in-law Anyone Could Ever Know. To My Younger Brother Stanley J. Thomas, Whos Memories Are Very Dear To My Heart. I Will Always Embrace His Desire To Be A Part Of Whatever I Was Involved In. Acknowledgement Is Also Given To Mother Ada McCrimmon, The Lady Of Min-*

*istry Who Was Most Instrumental And Responsible For My Being In Sylacauga, Alabama. May God Continue To Bless Her Memories And The Seeds She Planted. Last, But Not Least To My Mentor And Favorite Uncle, Lonnie Green, Jr., Who Initiated My Interest In The Martial Arts And The Art Of Positive Thinking And Self-control. I Will Always Hold His Teachings Close And Use Them As Part Of My Every Day Life!*

# INTRODUCTION

The Concept of the Stud VS Stallion is a phenomenon that challenges the notion that "all men are the same" and compares the views of two different mind-sets using as illustrations, two different horses of the same family and comparing them to the images of the 21st Century male.

I will begin my illustration with "talking horses".

Imagine two horses talking to each other, the Stud to the Stallion. "Hey man have you seen the way those humans look at me. Have you seen those clothes they wear and the way they wear their hair? Have you noticed the way they treat their children and relatives? Have you noticed those things they ride in and how they wash them? Boy, I bet it feels great when they apply that soap and water and then dry with a cloth. Have you notice the instruments they use to eat from? I bet all of that is nice to have. I wonder what it would take to have such nice things happen to me. I wonder what it is I must do to gain this type of treatment".

My mind suddenly reflects on the words of Moses, "I'd rather suffer affliction with the people of God than to enjoy the pleasures of sin for only a season". I believe that Moses was saying to us in today's terms; I would rather stay real and free than to be enslaved by the acquisition of a few clothes, shoes, fine cars and homes, and a crowd that affirms me only as long as I produce the things they demand.

The Stallion's reply; "Hey man, I don't have all those

things you are speaking of and I guess I never will if it means becoming as humans. I am a Stallion considered "wild" because I will not allow myself to be captured and taken over by the humans. I just can't allow myself to become what they are because I love being free and making my own decisions. If I am to have all of the nicer things in life as you say Mr. Stud, then that means I must become just what they want me to be and then they will use me as they will. I believe I would rather run and fight if I must to stay free. Being free allows me to help other leaders of the herd to reach maturity. Being free allows me to serve in the raising of the little ones of the herd. Being free allows me to eat when I desire to, not when someone else tells me "its time to eat". Being free allows me the opportunity to select the mate of my choice, not the mate of their choice. I may not receive all of the nice baths with selected soaps and cleansers; I may not have the nice stables to cover me from the rains and the winds. I may never have a leather saddle and warm blanket put on my back and grooming of my hair, but one thing I will have is my freedom".

# CHAPTER 1
## Freedom Vs Conformity

When I am free I can grow and mature from the inside, because from the inside is who and what I really am. I would rather nurture, mature and grow what I really am rather than what someone wants me to become. If I am to become what someone else wants me to be it will cause me much frustration and discomfort. I will be displeased and unpleasant to be around. I will have mood swings, good one day and not so good the next day. Why? It because I cannot be what I really am to know myself and grow myself to be what's inside of me. And Mr. Stud, if that's the life you desire to live then get ready for many unhappy days ahead. It's good to be able to relate with those things but if I am to have them, I will have them as a free Stallion and not an enslaved Stud. If I never have the "nicer things in life" one thing I will appreciate myself for and that is staying me.

You must learn to love a person for who they are and not for what you want them to be. I tell my daughter, "Kiss me because I am dad, not just because I gave you a little money." Love me for me not just for what I bring to the table or to the home. Love me as a person not as porcelain. This is difficult to do if one has been dictated to by external forces. Sometimes we try to please our own friends, mates and family according to the way we think others feel we should, but tell yourself, "it's not according to the approval of others that determines how I entreat my own friends, mate and family, it's from the inside, being who and what I really am. Being real is an inside job not an external overlay of opinions from others. Don't allow external pressure to cause you to be something you are not. You put yourself in the risky position of losing those who love you and love watching you as you mature into that greater person you can be. In most cases, a man can do greater things beyond what he is doing if he can get over the external opinions.

God speaks and deals with man internally because He knows that the polluted opinions from the external can distort man's understanding of what God is saying to him. Inside of you is where God abides and all conversations, instructions, etc. is happening inside you. Sometimes there is just too much external noise. I recall the time that I was showering and my wife call for me; she has a small quiet voice and she wall call from the top of her small little voice. I could not hear her for the noise of the shower. Once I finished showering and stopped the water flow, it was then I heard her calling. She did not raise her voice for she was already at the top level of voice volume the same as she was when she called me the first time. Now I hear her but I had to turn off the external noise. We need to turn off the external noise so we might hear the internal conversation that God is trying to have with us. I an fully persuaded that inner development is most important if we are to mature properly

Developing from the inside outward will bring about a greater respect and appreciation for the beauty of God's creation and one will strive to live and enjoy the abundant life that God has created for us opposed to frequent complaints. I do believe if one could mature past uncontrollable lust "strong desires" the appreciation of one another's strength, knowledge and skill will be manifested. I have found men who cannot enjoy the beauty of the opposite sex due to his desire to have a sexual encounter with her. A woman should not feel as though she has to be on the take or "hit on" every time she encounters a so-called compliment from a man. She should not have to defend her beauty but enjoy the appreciated compliments of a man. Men have a great work ahead but must overcome the Stud mentality. A Stud mentality wants to breed and not lead. I feel that the Stud approach has caused men to look at women as just sexual opportunities and have hindered men's ability to appreciate the beauty of her strength. Women possesses a powerful inner strength that accompanies great men to success, only if he can appreciate her strength and not feel threatened by it and does not attempt to destroy it by trying to force her to be something she is not.

A woman is not made for sex only, "breeding" as some men think; instead she possesses the abilities and skills for leading. Consider the virtuous woman in the book of Proverbs verses 10-31, she became the leader to her family without taking over the husband's position. An appreciative man will always make a path for the assistance of his strong wife and not feel threatened by her strength. Yet, he admires her beauty and appreciates the beauty God gave her and shares with him to enjoy. Speaking derogatory toward her will not eradicate who she really is, for the true women is inside, despite of how much she expresses herself hypocritically to please the man. Allow her to be herself and help her develop her true inner personally so she may be of great assistance and appreciation to you. She wants to feel one of a special selection, not just someone picked up from the open streets. And when the approach is that "I just want to have you for a few minutes of pleasure, to her this is an insult to her spirituality and intelligence.

The Stallion in the wild has the freedom to allow growth

from the inner spirit that will result in knowing who and what he is. He will mature in his ability to lead and make ways for other leading horses without the feel of being threatened. There is a great lesson to learn from this concept of the Stud-Stallion and the Wild-Stallion. Remember, both are male horses but only one has been domesticated to the will of humans or may I say "the external forces."

# CHAPTER 2
# Nature of the Species

Horses are eager to please their owners or trainers. Most horses have good memories and can easily be trained to obey commands. A horse may learn to come when its owner whistles. A circus horse takes "bows" when its trainer touches its front legs with a whip. Horses can learn to respond to even the slightest signals. People who watch when experts ride on well-trained horses often cannot see these signs. For example, the horse moves forward when the rider's legs are pressed lightly against the horse's side. It turns at a touch of the reins against its neck. The quick obedience of the horse has helped make it one of our most valuable animals.

People have improved the natural qualities of the horse by breeding various kinds of horses. For example, horse raisers can breed a fast horse with a strong horse to produce a animal that has both speed and power.

Each of the three main groups of horses has many breeds. However, a single breed may include horses of more than one type:

**Colt**, technically, is a male horse less than 4 years old. However, the word colt is often used for any young horse.

**Filly** is a female horse less than 4 years old.

**Crossbred** means bred from a sire of one breed and a dam of another.

**Dam** is the mother of a foal.

**Foal** is either a newborn male or a newborn female horse.

**Gelding** is male horse that cannot be used for breeding because it has had some of its reproductive organs removes.

**Mare** is a female horse more than 4 years old.

**Mustang** is the wild horse of the western plains, descended from Spanish horses.

**Purebred** means bred from horses that are of the same breed.

**Sire** is the father of a foal.

**Stallion** is the male horse that can be used for breeding, but not all the time the case.

**Stud** is a male horse used for breeding

On breeding farms, stallions and mares are carefully selected for mating on the basis of their ancestry and physical qualities. Breeders of race horses also consider the racing records of the animals. A Champion racing stallion may earn

## STALLION OR STUD?

millions of dollars for the owner in stud fees. By using the horse for breeding purposes a stud fee is paid to a stallion's owner for the use of the stallion to sire (father) a Foal (newborn male or female horse). Breeding horses is not an exact science. Breeders can never be completely certain of producing a colt or filly of champion quality.

Most breeders mate their mares to a stallion in spring. The mares give birth about springtime the following year. People who raise race horses want their foals to be born as soon as possible after January 1because the foals will be considered yearlings the following January. A foal that is born early in the year has more time to grow and develop before the races as a 2-year old.   A foal stays with its mother for the first six months after birth. The owner then weans (separates) the foal from its mother and puts it out to pasture with other foals.
*Source: World Book Encyclopedia*

# CHAPTER 3
# The Stud
# Role, Characteristics and Traits of a Breeder

As I write this chapter, I consider the young men that believe sex is the essence of manhood (Stud). My study of the stud concept will hopefully help you to understand that sex (breeding) is not the ultimate or essential attribute of being a man. Being a stud does not equip you (one) nor prepare you for the responsibilities of being the man needed to lead and excel in today's society.

Look at the stud concept. He is first a male with a purpose. His main purpose is to breed, not lead. He is owned by someone that thrives through the sell of the stud's reproduction services. The stud is forced to submit to the one who owns him and is to serve his master (owner) and fulfill the wishes of his master. He awaits a different mare frequently for the purpose of breeding, not leading. He does not have the privilege of selecting a specific mare that would foal a colt of his desire. He just breeds her and gets ready for the next mare that is brought in to him. He is enjoys breeding but there is never a commitment to neither the mare nor the foal after breeding. He breeds and leaves. The responsibility of raising the foal is left to the mare. The stud does not assume the responsibility of protecting, feeding, sheltering nor leading the mare nor his foal. His job is finished. He has bred.

The stud lives a sheltered life in that he is protected by his owner from the free world with limited pasture, limited barn space, etc., so that he is available to fulfill his owner's purpose for ownership, impregnating mares. He is feed by his owner and never seeks his own food, water or a place to live. The one who owns him dictates his life. He is left without any rights or responsibility for the family he has produced.

The stud is painted into a box. He has the tendency to judge life from the box he is painted into. If you are boxed in and never acquire the experience of being responsible for others especially those who are a part of you or your offspring then it will be difficult for you to judge justly those who acquire such responsibilities.

So many young men believe or feel that being a stud (sowing their wild oats) or getting' with every female that is receptive of uncommitted sexual encounters, makes them popular. It may; however, the consequences of this irresponsible, risky behavior can and most often will result irreversible or detrimental consequences that will have a negative effect on you for a lifetime. Regardless of how accepting society may be and no matter how glamorous the media paints the picture, uncommitted sexual acts result in sexually transmitted disease, some incurable, unwanted, premature pregnancy and child birth, child support payments one cannot escape, broken hearts, and emotional scars that take a life time to heal. A leader (the stallion) realizes that sexual promiscuity (being a stud) is detrimental or counter productive to any plan he has for a successful future. The stud does not look ahead to his future, all that matters is sex. He does not consider the consequences or the responsibility of sex.

There are horse breeders that own studs that breed into artificial containers that simulate the female horse. The stud has no knowledge that it is not a real horse. His sperm is drawn out transplanted into a live mare through artificial insemination. The stud never knows he has produced an offspring.

My friends, James and Jackie Hale, helped me to understand this concept. Get the seed from the stud and keep the stud up for the next available and receptive mare. What is the mentality of the stud? Breeding day after day. The only diet he needs is to insure he has the strength for breeding. He does not have to run through any canyons, up any hills, through any rivers, just breed and leave. He does not have to find shelter for anyone, he trust his owner will provide. He does not have to help raise any of his foals; the mare will see to that. He does not even know if they do not survive nor does he care. Have sex and be happy. He is satisfied through fulfillment of his own pleasurable, selfish desire. Give it up girl; I am a **Stud!**

A Stud has no sense of commitment. There has never been a reason for him to do so. His master commits himself to insuring the stud's basic needs are met and that the mare cares for the foal. So many young men have created this type situation for the parents to maintain and sustain shunning their responsibility for children they produced. They brag about how many young ladies they have sex with and even impregnated and leave the responsibility on the young lady and her parents or on his parents. Once you become a father it is your responsibility to sustain that you have created. If you feel you are not ready to accept the responsibility of caring and providing for another human life, you should act responsibly and not engage in the act that creates life. Being a stud is nothing to brag about. Being a stud is actually a selfish, shameful and sinful act against God and man. In the realm of human life, it should be unlawful to breed and not lead.

# CHAPTER 4
# The Stallion
# The Characteristics, Role and Traits of a Leader

In the wild the Stallion is the leader and considered one of the greatest horses a man can ever own. He is independent and responsible for his herd as well as his offspring. A stallion is selective of the mare he wishes to breed. He is not painted into a box. He is concerned with the present generation and the generation to come. He seeks for a strong mare to breed so that he may produce a strong foal like himself. Strong men (Stallions) are not intimidated by strong women. A strong woman is a blessing to a strong man spiritually, physically, and emotionally in the production of a family, business or ministry. A stallion will not breed to a mare just because she is available and receptive. He is very selective of the mare he wishes to breed with; unlike the stud who will breed with anyone that is receptive. The stallion will select the one he desires to foal his colt. He seeks qualities that will strengthen the herd for generations to come. The stallion is strong and responsible and he seeks to reproduce a foal that possesses those same characteristics.

A Stallion is one that understands the importance of having and keeping a strong mare in his herd. He does not force her to do all of the raising of the foal, he shares in that responsibility. Society has carved out roles that nourishes a double standard and staggered mindsets that there are one set of rules for the woman and a different set of rules for the man as it relates to child rearing and house work. I am persuaded that if men are the true leaders then it is our responsibility to learn all that is necessary to be the leader. Who said that it is the woman's job to do all of the cooking, washing, and helping children with school work. Why should the woman bear all of the responsibility of paying the bills, making the arrangements with the creditors, etc?

I am strongly persuaded that every good and strong leading man should know or be willing to learn how to prepare meals, clean the house, iron the clothes, and assist the children with school work and still maintain his lawn and household repairs. If you are to be the leader, then be the leader in every aspect of family life. A leader should be able to enhance his spouse and increase her skills or knowledge base by sharing with her in some area where she may not be as knowledgeable. A stallion will give her a rest; help keep her strong not just in her mind but her body as well. By doing so, you increase the likelihood that she will feel like doing more for you willingly and without you asking. You are the man and you are called to lead, not boss but lead! Anyone can boss and give orders; however, the sign of a true leader is one who can and is ensample to his family and is willing and able to carry out the orders he is giving. A stallion leads at all times. He plans and prepares ahead. When there is danger, he has located a safe haven prior to the danger and he leads his followers to that safe place. He can't do this sitting around waiting on his mare to do everything. The stallion is always seeking for food, higher plains and security from the storm. When he senses a storm he rounds up his herd and insists that they follow him and they are confident enough in him that he will do the right thing for them. When you have proven that you are capable of

## STALLION OR STUD?

making good decisions for your family, it will not be a problem for them to trust you and follow you. You cannot acquire the skills and ability to be a sound decision maker, if you are always depending on your spouse to make the decisions while you give orders after the decisions have been made. A stallion is always making decisions, not making all decisions. He is not just standing around waiting for someone to decide for him or his herd. He is always looking forward and planning ahead for whatever event that may occur.

A stallion will not leave his family out in the storm or in harms way and run to cover him. He will be the last to go into a cave or a covered canyon after his entire herd and family are safe and covered. He watches over his herd while they are grazing in pasture to be sure that they are protected from the dangers that surrounds them. If there is an attack on the herd, the stallion will leave his watch post to rush to their defense even if it means giving up his life to save theirs. The bible tells us that we should be willing to give our life for our family even as Christ gave his for the Church.

Leaders are not intimidated by the opinions of others. A leader posses different characteristics than the breeder and has a different mode of operation. A leader is not dependent upon a owner to supply his needs, but is independent and assumes the responsibility of insuring the needs of others are met. The stud conforms to the owner and fleshly desire, because he is not interdependent (in a committed relationship) and is insecure.

In the book and movie "Roots" by Alex Haley, the slave Kunta Kinte, lost his foot because he was a leader who was accustom to being free and making his own decisions. He was not accustomed to submitting to ownership. He lost his foot because he refused to give up his original name. He eventually gave in to the pain and suffering caused by the slave master but inwardly he never gave in. He was still free inside, despite the confinement and affliction of his physical body. When you are a true leader, people who do not respect independence and individuality may not like you. As a leader it is your responsibility to use sound judgment to make good, wise decisions for yourself and your followers.

Leaders love to be in the company of other leaders and are not intimidated by the strength of the other. Leaders realize that "iron sharpens iron" (KJV Proverbs 27:17).

Other horses always surround a stallion. They enjoy being around him. Things, barns, trees, pastures and people not of his kind surround a stud.

When you are leading, you are always under the criticism of others. They are often under the impression that their views are superior to yours but they are not leading and they cannot see what you can see. Because of this, you may be alone and in a very uncomfortable season of life. Sometimes there are no places or no one to go to for help. It is at those times that you must rely on your instincts and experiences. Your confidence gained through previous trials, triumphs and successes will give you a sense of knowing that your decision is the correct one.

Leaders cannot afford to be moved with every contrary or negative comment nor the opinions of those under their leadership. As a leader, you will learn to resolve hurts and emotional pain quickly so that these emotions do not fester and hinder you from accomplishing those things you have in view. Getting focused and staying focused are necessary skills for a leader. Don't ever stray from your path and lose your focus. In the end, you will be rewarded by intensifying your aim and doubling your efforts. You will reap if you don't faint. We cannot lose sight on our responsibility as the stallion, a leader.

# STALLION OR STUD?

Not the stud, a breeder. In spite of the difficulties we will face, staying focused requires maturity and is a sign of growth.

It is important for us to understand that as leaders we do not have the luxury of playing immature games while trying to lead others through serious matters in life. Paul said "when I was a child I understood as a child, I acted a child and I thought as a child, but when I became a man (mature) I put away child like games. This is to say, he made mature, responsible decisions that would benefit those who followed him. It is not the easiest place to be in life but it is rewarding to see those you are leading prosper. He does not play child-like games. He is always thinking of ways to improve his situation and that of others.

A stallion is always aware of his surroundings and his daily destiny. Rarely does he allow anything or anyone to cause him to lose focus on his destiny or interfere with his plans. Because of this, many stud minded people do not understand the mindset of a stallion. A stallion is always reminded of his purpose and the care of his herd.

A stallion is one that many find pleasure in being around. They are inspired by his intelligence and motivated by his actions. They enjoy watching him make possible things that are impossible to those not of his kind (a stud). Many times he is criticized because he is not drawn away to folly. He is one of the most important horses in the herd and the most sought after.

The stallion (leader) will seek for the medicine for the herd. This means, he has no master to turn to for aid. He must go out into the dangerous terrain to find the right plants and grass that will help heal the sick members of his herd. When they are thirsty he must lead them to water. When their feeding ground becomes desolate, he must lead them to greener pasture so that they are fed. This includes the mare of his foal and the foal. A stallion's job is a twenty-four hour responsibility. It takes accountability, commitment, and self-denial to produce or provide these necessities and to accomplish a purpose. Development of the qualities and implementation of the role demonstrated by the stallion can ignite and produce change in those observing a man fulfilling his obligations. This type leadership will result on positive outcomes in the households of men all over this nation. Brethren, stop being colts and let's assume our role as stallions.

# CHAPTER 5
# Doomed to Stud or Destined to be a Stallion

*Comment: Habits take time to develop. Remember that your character is the sum total of your habits. You can't claim to be kind unless you are habitually kind. You show kindness without even thinking about it. You can't claim to have integrity unless it is your habit to always be honest.*

Interestingly enough a Stud is a Stallion but of a different mind-set and purpose. Both the Stud and Stallion are male in gender; however characteristically their behavior is different. A Stud is a stallion that has been domesticated to breed pursuant to the desire and gain of his owner. A Stud-Stallion's freedom to function freely what he truly is has been taken away. Through my studies, I have learned that a Stud-Stallion is not pleasant around other horses. This is not surprising considering he has been taken away from his natural environment and other free horses and their territory to run, lead and make decisions without the influence of people.

The Stud-Stallion has become a slave to his owner, to say the least; he does not have decisions to make. He is led by the order of the one desiring his service. Sometimes we lose sight on our inner ability to perform great things for God because there are people who desire our services without giving respect to the power that lies within us. If we allow others to cause us to lose focus on our inner abilities and capabilities then we are as weak as the Stud-Stallion. This will result in being in a breeding place rather than a leading place.

Once we are given to a particular assignment, then the perfecting classes begin. These classes are given to make one better at what he or she is called to perform. Practice makes perfect, even if it is a perfect wrong. If you practice wrong you will perfect the practice and your character will form to whatever you practice. Take the Stallion out of the wild and domesticate him and practice with him what it is that you wish for him to do and he will become perfect doing it. His mind-set will be transformed to that of the owners even though he is not a human he senses that he should have some of the same benefits stemming from the prior treatment he received for the services he rendered for his owner. You can tell by his behavior, he wants concession for doing what he feels pleases his owner. You will find this among several different animals, not just the horse.

*Comment: There is only one way to develop the habits of Christ-like character. You must practice them and that takes time. There are no instant habits.*

Growth is a painful experience. There is no maturity "growth" without change. One must be willing to suffer losing something from the past. You must let go of past experiences. At times we feel afraid of losing our image or the image we have portrayed to hide the pain and wounds received from various experiences that have not yet healed. Instead we depict a face of being healed but the pain within drives us into areas that divulge the hurting areas in our life.

I believe that the Stud has difficulty dealing with change

## STALLION OR STUD?

more than dealing with the people around him. He still has the urge to be himself and free, and must deal with letting go of what he is accustom to particularly the freedom to choose where he will reign. He must struggle with his desire to run free or walk with his head up in the clouds experiencing the fresh breeze on a windy day. No halter, no saddle, no blanket, no rider adding weight to his back, just free to choose his desires of the day. No one to force him to go in a direction contrary to his own will. Just imagine yourself being forced to give up your freedom to become somewhat of a slave just for a few minutes of pleasure day after day. Can you see yourself being put in a position of unlearning? Everything you have learned from a youth to an adult comes under the scrutiny of the one (s) that desire you to be just what they want you to be; even if it means breaking your free spirit to be domesticated and "controlled by others."

*Comment: It's important to know that there are controlling spirits and you need to be aware of them so they can be broke.*

When you are taken out of your natural environment and natural habits are relinquished one should expect a different response. That response is usually one of anger, disagreement, stubbornness and reluctance to learn new habits without concession. In many cases one is given to concession for services and/or adaptation. Consider this as payment for conforming to what other desire of you. You have been bought with their price.

We should be like the Stallion of the wild, "run for your freedom." Before I sell my freedom for pleasure, I will run away from the mediocrity that conforms me to be what others desire me to be if it is not who I really am. I may not make all of the right decisions but the decisions I make are mine. I cannot prepare for the next generation if I am dictated to by someone who will not allow me to be the true me. The Stallion of the wild understands that he is driven by spirit on the inside and not by external pressure from others. To prepare for the future one must realize that it is an inside job.

*Even the enemy knows how important it is to operate from the inside!*

Consider these verses of scripture:

### Isaiah 59:19
So shall they fear the Name of the Lord from the west and His glory from the rising of the sun. When the enemy shall come *in* like a flood, the spirit of the Lord shall lift up a standard against Him.

### Job 1:7
And the Lord said unto Satan, whence comest thou? Then Satan answered the Lord, and said, From going to and fro *in* the earth, and from walking up and down *in* it.

### Matthew 12:29
... or else how can one enter *into* a strong man's house, and spoil his goods, except he first bind the strong man? And then he will spoil his house.

### St. John 7:37- 38
In the last day, that great day of the feast, Jesus stood and cried, saying, if any man thirst, let him come *unto* me and drink.

## STALLION OR STUD?

He that believeth on me, as the scripture hath said, *out of his belly shall flow rivers of living waters.*

*Comment: Notice that "out of his belly" suggesting that the rivers of living waters came from the inside!*

### St. John 4:14
But whosoever drinketh of the water that I shall give him shall never thirst; but the water that I shall give him shall be *in* him a well of water springing up into everlasting life.

### St John 15:7
If ye abide *in* me and my words abide *in* you, ye shall ask what ye will, and it shall be done unto you.

### I John 4:4
Ye are of God, little children, and have overcome them: because greater is He that is *in* you, than he that is in the world.

The words we tell ourselves are more important than we realize. If you tell yourself something enough times and in the right circumstances, you will believe those words whether true or not. We must be mindful of the word "advice" you give. In many instances, we give positive subjects with negative connotations. By doing this you cannot be yourself. You must mask your true identity.

Talk to yourself. Self talk is the words we tell ourselves in our thoughts. The words we process in our minds about ourselves, about other people, experiences, life in general, God, the future, the past, the present. Self talk is specifically, all of the words you say to yourself all of the time.

But I say unto you, "if no one around you encourages you", "tell yourself the truth." Tell yourself what God said...The Truth. Romans 3:4, says, "Let God be true and every man a lie". Say what He says, until you see what he said.

Some ask "why do I feel the way I do?" Typically, he or she wants to put the blame on something or someone else. "It's my wife, she's the one who makes me feel the way I do," or "it's my husband's fault." "My job isn't satisfying me" or "my friends are disappointing," or "my children are a disappointment." Some people blame their problems on their church. They find fault with their Pastor. They complain that people aren't friendly enough or that everyone else in the world is a hypocrite.

Some say "I am alone," nobody loves me or cares about me. Nobody wants to be with me. I'm rejected and useless.

Tell yourself the truth. *Say what He says until you see what He said:*

**Untruth:**
I can't make it

**Truth:**
Luke 1:37: for with God nothing shall be impossible

**Untruth:**
I am alone, I've lost all my friends, I am disturbed, I am lost

**Truth**
Philippians 4:8-9: Finally, brethren whatsoever things are true, whatsoever things are honest,

whatsoever things are just, whatsoever things are pure, whatsoever things are lovely, whatsoever things are of good report: if there be any virtue, and if there be any praise, think on these things. These things, which ye have both learned, and received, and heard, and seen in me; do: and the God of peace shall be with you.

We need to get up and off our pity wagons. Use each situation as an opportunity to go inside and tell ourselves the truth and watch the truth work from the inside through to the outside. We must say to our obstacles that we are more than conquerors and to our sickness, that by His stripes we are healed, and to our weaknesses, I am strong. Yes some things are reality and situations are true, but everything that is true is not the truth. Jesus said, "I am the way the truth and the life."

# CHAPTER 6
## Leaving a Legacy

The foal or colt is to be supervised by the stallion not the stallion by the foal or colt. Many times men are expressing themselves as the son (s). But what is desired and needful is that men will stand up and take hold of their children and lead them in wisdom, truth and the righteousness of God. If we are to turn the country back to God, then we must become stallions and leave the studding alone. So the responsible thing for you and your family, stop being selfish and irresponsible toward your children and family, stand up and be independent and not dependent of others. You have the power to make a difference in the live of everyone you come in contact with.

Commitment and devotion are important to those God has given you. Don't just breed and leave. But be devoted to it to assure that it will grow properly and be nurtured correctly. Come out of your painted box believing that the entire world is the color of your box, trust me, it's not. Learn and be educated about your duties and responsibilities as a man first and then a husband before you try to be a father. You cannot instruct properly if you are a man try to display boyhood. If you missed that part of your life, remember, you cannot go back and recover that without confusing where you are with what you are trying to be. Wherever you are in your life, learn to appreciate that area and do all you can to discover everything you need to know about it. If you have children then you cannot be the child. If you are an adult without children, remember, you cannot be mama's little boy any longer. You are a man now and you must make mature decisions that men make. Be responsible for you actions and stop blaming others for your shortcomings, and if you make a mistake, own up to it, confess and get over it like men do. Don't hold on to it discussion it, just confess it and go on, for life doesn't stop just because one makes a mistake. Life is filled with mistakes, in most cases of a success story; there was first a mistake then success. Remember, you are not breeding, you are leading and where and how you lead is very, very important to the followers. It's not just you and you alone anymore, but you have others looking to you for advice and leadership. Someone have need of you gift, your expertise and our strength, so, don't beat up on yourself, find yourself, strengthen yourself, educate yourself and become the leader and not the breeder. Be the stallion and not the stud.

We must identify with our hurts which means that we must understand that it is not weakness to cry sometime. Yes! Real men cry, but we do not drown in our tears. We must learn to express our feelings without being domination to the family or spouse. We are dominate without being dominating. This is where the appreciation of a strong woman is important. A strong woman will understand your hurts and crying without degrading our manhood. We must learn to be tough not rough. Tough people experience hurt just as fragile people. Nothing is wrong or weak with expressing your true feelings, without doing so you will never experience true deliverance and healing from your hurt. You are not commanded to hypocrite trying to be someone that you are not or to act like someone that you are not. There are customized trials just for you and on the flip side of that, there are customized blessing just for you also.

# STALLION OR STUD?

You cannot receive blessing designed for someone else just as though you cannot suffer the trials that's designed for someone else. Go through your trial then only you can wear the custom blessing that God has in store for you. Never envy the things of others for you have no idea of their trials they have suffered just to enjoy the pleasures of their blessings.

As leader, we will have many trials, but God will bring us through them, and let us never say that I'll just quit, for quitting is not the nature of a stallion. He will lead until he just can't lead anymore, but he will never look back to quit, he'll just die leading or trying to lead.

Leaders pass on to the next generation a journal filled with wisdom and their experiences. He will not take his experiences to the grave without revelation of the benefit to the next beneficiaries. A wise leader leaves a legacy for others to build upon sharing with those following him how he came thus far. Take the time to share with those you are leading and train them to share with those whom they will lead. This takes an unselfish, mature act of character and spirit and is so very important for the ongoing knowledge for the next generation and the strength of the next generation.

If you are a breeder (stud) only, your mind will not be directed in this area of keeping the generation going long and strong. All you are concern about is the next mare which is ready to breed or have sex. Studs don't truly care about an ongoing generation, for his babies are scatted and he has no knowledge of there whereabouts. That's not his nature anyway, he doesn't have that responsibility of commitment and devotion to the things he assisted in creating, he's satisfied knowing that another good feeling is coming up soon. His offspring doesn't even know their siblings due to no commitment and devotion to the family by the father. A mother can raise up a good son but it takes a man to raise up a man. Iron sharpens Iron. (Proverbs 27:17)

If you comprehend the concept of a stud, notice that his owner is concerned more about his offspring than he is. The master even makes money from the sell of his baby. Consider the child welfare and foster care system this country. Children are left behind by their fathers and mothers and are placed in the system for State agencies to find homes for them. The government pays a stranger to care for the child and bring the child to adulthood. The sad part is the child is still often left without committed relationships or a strong support system. Basically we are replicating the actions of the stud by producing offspring (breeding) and relinquishing the responsibility of raising them to a stranger. Someone is paid to raise your child or children while you move on to the next fleshly pleasure (be that pleasure, sex, drugs or unrighteous living). The child never gets to know you as he/she grows into adulthood. He takes on the spirit of the stud master and not the true sire. And we have questions why our generation is so confused and lack security and confidence about who they are. I believe that this is one of the reasons for the today's identity crisis". We desire for our generation to be secure with who they are and to be the best of who they are. But, if they are not connected with their true self, their roots, then confusion sets in. Fathers, your babies need you to lead them, instruct them, love and protect them. They are your offspring. Nurture and protect your own. Don't leave them for the "system", the prisons, drugs, prostitution, crime and the grave. The "system" and the graves are rich enough with gifts that were never manifested and shared within our communities. We are stallions! Let us take hold of our herds and foal to deposit into them those things that are good and necessary for success today and tomorrow.

# STALLION OR STUD?

Leaders observe how well their offspring respond under certain conditions to determine if they possess the skills to survive. If he feels that the offspring may be overtaken by a particular condition or situation, he will give support where needed. He will not let the foal fall to fatality. He will give his life before he allows the life of the foal to be taken. The stallion wishes only the best for his offspring, and in order to insure that, he must be present and with him during his young years and remain with him until he becomes strong enough and experienced enough to stand alone. God will likewise allow us to go through very hard trials, but He is there for us, to support us, to assure that no weapon formed against us prospers, and when we go through the fire it does not kindle against us and through the floods they do not overtake us. (KJV Isaiah 54:17 and Isaiah 43:2).

God is always concerned about us because we are his children and he cares for. Remember, anything God allows, He will do something about it. Don't ever surrender due to a trial or a test. Just know that the experience from the trial will educate you, and you can share your experience with your foal. Remember the Stallion, he shares with his offspring to make him aware of the things that may come upon him. He teaches him how to make wise and responsible decisions and teaches him the value of staying focused on each day's destiny!

# CHAPTER 7
# Men What Can We Do?

I am sure there are men who seek to know what we can do to change the socially accepted stud behaviors. We are not pleased with those behaviors and neither is God. These type behaviors can be detrimental to our relationships with our families, our spouses and most of all our relationship with God. We need and want to prevent the problems caused by such behaviors because of the hurt and pain they inflict to us as individuals and to our society.

Prayer, the word of God and education are the keys to preventing these acts. To control negative results is to change human behavior. The EDA's of ones character influences their behavior. The EDA's are:

> E—motions are specific feelings such has anger, sadness, happiness, hurt, disappointment.
> D—esire is to intensely long for something
> A—fection meaning your mental or emotional state

Life has what I call the "MD's". Motivation and Discipline. As strange as it may seem, life has a way to motivate you and also to Discipline you. Motivation is a will to act. A law of Physics says for every action there is an equal and opposite reaction. Discipline is training that develops self-control, character and order of efficiency.

Sometimes we just have to be still and know that God is God.

Let's consider motivation. There are seven steps I use to motivate others:

1. Tell them what you want them to do
2. Tell them why you want it done
3. Show them
4. Delegate them
5. Observe them
6. Catch them doing something right
7. Praise progress

There are three essential keys to motivation that is included with the seven keys and they are: (1) What (2) Why (3) Feedback.

As leaders in our homes and our communities, these steps and keys are very important to the success of our personal and home life as well as our business and life in our community. Why? Because statistics say, 83 percent of a your learning is through sight, 11 percent of your learning is through hearing, 31 percent of your learning is through smell, 1 percent of your learning is through taste and 1 percent of your learning is through feel or touch. These same statistics state that the average person remembers 10 percent of what is read, 20 percent of what you tell them and 30 percent of what they see. 70 percent of what we say to ourselves is remembered.

This means "ye shall have whatsoever you say" by 70 percent.

The knowledge gained through hearing is 11 percent with 2 percent retained; the knowledge gained through sight is 83 percent with 30 percent retained. This is a total of 94 percent of our knowledge gained and 32 percent retained.

# STALLION OR STUD?

What is my point? My point is that if I tell you, you will forget it. If I show you, you will remember it. But if I involve you, you will understand it. If we are to change the course of life for our children and communities, we must get involved. We must be active participants in changing behaviors that are and have been detrimental to our success. It is important to practice that which you wish to be a leader of. To be a great Stud, you must be involved and practice the behaviors of a Stud. But if you are to be a great Stallion and I mean a free Stallion (a leader), then you must maintain the freedom of your God given purpose and not conform to the external pressures of the world's standards. Responsibility is a choice. The choice is yours! Are you a Stud or a Stallion?

# ABOUT THE AUTHOR:

Bishop Marshal L. Thomas is the Founder and Presiding Bishop of the Pentecostal Fellowship Churches, Inc. He resides in the small, but growing town of Chelsea, Alabama. He pastors in Sylacauga, Alabama. He is also the President of the P.F.C. Bible Institute. He has received several academic degrees including a PhD in Psychology, ThD., MBS, LL.D, MA in music, and a BS in civil engineering. Through the efforts of Dun & Bradstreet (NYSE: DNB) he has been enlisted into the National Register of Who's Who among Executives, Professionals and Businessmen 2004 edition. He enjoys horseback riding, skydiving, scuba diving, practicing the martial arts, quiet times outside, and time with his family. Bishop Thomas believes in a balanced lifestyle, sound body, soul and spirit. His greatest passion is preaching and teaching the Word of God.